Forever Dancing

Story By
Joan Hope MacNaughton

Illustrations by
Janniche Dyrø

This book is dedicated to the children of dance throughout the world. May you always feel the spirit.

To my wonderful father and mother who always gave me unconditional love and courage.

Hugs to my husband, Donald, who knew I would be forever dancing.

And especially to my daughter, Samantha, who was born dancing. Take the gift of my heart, may you be forever dancing through life with my love.

My gratitude to Felix and Rebecca for their faith in my story.
—**Joan Hope MacNaughton**

These illustrations are dedicated to my niece, Emma. She is almost five years old and started ballet some months ago. She told me she wanted to become a dancer when she grows up.
I told her she already is, and if she keeps dancing, she definitely will. I hope this book will keep her inspired and remembering her wish.
—**Janniche Dyrø**

Forever dancing is the author's true story. In the story, she describes her development as a dancer and ultimately as a dance teacher whose mission is to bring to children and youth the special gift of joy and happiness that dance carries. The author is the owner of Leggz Ltd. dance studio, located in Rockville Centre, New York.

Forever Dancing

Story by Joan Hope MacNaughton
Illustrations by Janniche Dyrø

LCCN 2004092282 (English Version)
LCCN 2004092283 (Spanish Version)

ISBN 0-9675413-8-7 (English Version)
ISBN 0-9675413-9-5 (Spanish Version)

First Edition Printed in Hong Kong.

Publisher's Cataloging-in-Publication
(Provided by Quality Books, Inc.)

MacNaughton, Joan Hope.
    Forever dancing / story by Joan Hope MacNaughton ;
illustration by Janniche Dyro.
        p. cm.
    SUMMARY: A dancer tells of her life from her first
dance class to her current ownership of a dance studio,
explaining that the art of dance is more than the simple
execution of particular steps and body movements. It is
her way to tell a story from the heart.
    LCCN 2004092282
    ISBN 0-9675413-8-7

    1. Dancers--Juvenile fiction. [1. Dancers--Fiction.
2. Dance--Fiction.]   I. Dyro, Janniche. II. Title.

PZ7.H7726For 2004   [E]
                                QBI33-2095

I am a dancer! My journey as a dancer has been one of my greatest joys. Dancing has helped me in so many ways. Through it, I have grown not only as a dancer but also as a human being. I have learned so much about life through dance. I am grateful for having dance as my lifelong teacher.

Here is my story.

I started dancing at the age of seven. I was encouraged by my mother and father who truly loved music and dance. There was always music playing in our house. My mother was a dancer. And my father was a self-taught musician. He played piano, cornet, accordion, and harmonica.

It was important to my parents that I carry on their tradition of dance and their love of music. My parents had steadfast belief in me. I was a star in their eyes. They never once doubted my ability. They were always telling me that I had a special gift. Dancing was it!

My journey began the very first day of dance class. I was very nervous. I did not know the teacher or any of the kids in my class. I did not even know if I could become a good dancer. My mother, however, insisted that I go.

Before the first class started, my mother bought my ballet slippers from my teacher. I loved my new dance shoes. They were such a pretty pink, and the leather was soft to the touch. Still, I really did not want to go into that dance room. It looked so big. But my mother simply said, "You're going in, and that's that." She turned me towards the door and sent me off with a gentle push.

I stepped nervously onto the floor. A musty smell filled the large room. Miss June, my teacher, seemed very serious. She did not say much. She just lined us up in first position. The next thing I knew, the pianist started playing on Miss June's cue, and I was dancing.

I tried as hard as I could to do everything right. I did exactly what Miss June told me to do. I did not talk or play. I just danced!

At first, I was a little scared to be in Miss June's class. But after a while, all my fears just melted away. I was having so much fun dancing. By the time class was over, I felt so proud of myself. I did it! I knew then that I loved to dance, and I could not wait to dance again.

The dance studio was a very special place. It was run by a famous vaudeville team of dancers. Between 1870 and 1920, vaudeville was the most popular form of entertainment in America. It was performed in theaters on Broadway and around the country. People went to these shows to feel happy, sad, silly, or amazed. They were never disappointed. Vaudevillians were quite simply the best performers around. They were talented singers, musicians, dancers, comedians, jugglers, magicians, and acrobats.

My vaudevillian teachers taught me that dance is more than just movements of the body. It is also a way to express feelings. I learned that people go to dance performances to connect with these feelings and to enjoy the beautiful techniques. I learned that dance can tell a story of happiness and joy, or one of pain and sorrow. My job as a dancer is to feel this story line and deliver it to the audience. Then they can feel it, too.

I spent a lot of time in dance training. I was taking classes four days a week after school for up to three hours. My family lived in a town near the dance studio. Since my mother did not drive, I had to walk to and from dance class. Each way was a forty-minute walk.

I was so committed to my training. I attended all my classes. I did not want to miss a thing. I was always on time, always warmed up after the long walk, and ready to give it my all on the dance floor.

This is what I did after school for as long as I can remember. I would see other kids in my school just hanging out with nothing to do. I felt so lucky to have such a special place to go. I felt lucky to be pursuing my dream.

I must say there were days when I did not feel like going to dance class. Especially when I had a bad day at school or did not feel well. I would leave school feeling tense and upset. These feelings would not last long though, because as soon as I entered the dance studio, I started to feel better. I put on my dance clothes, tightened my shoes, and stretched my tense muscles. Before I knew it, I was in my dance groove.

Once class started, the rest of the tension in my body went away as I concentrated only on my dance technique. Soon enough, I forgot all my worries. I was dancing my problems away! For me, the dance floor was a place of healing where my troubles always seemed to magically disappear.

I took as many classes as I could. I was in tap, jazz, ballet, pointe, (or "toe dancing,"), and even acrobatics. I knew that to succeed, I needed to be well-rounded in all areas of dance, especially ballet. Ballet is the foundation for most dance. It helped me develop good posture and strong, limber muscles, and it taught me excellent technique such as graceful arm work and intricate turns.

Ballet was the hardest for me, particularly the pointe classes, where I learned to dance on the tips of my toes in specially made pointe shoes with hard tips. I started pointe at the age of ten. That was when my teachers felt I was ready. Dancing on pointe made my feet sore. I had to learn to dance through the pain. My Russian ballet teacher's words still ring in my ears: "Pull up; get up on those toes." I did just that, and I am so glad I did. Ballet was essential to my training.

Tap was my favorite dance. It brought me so much joy. It came so naturally to me. I loved it! As soon as I put on the black shoes with metal taps on the heels and toes, and started tapping, my heart raced and my spirit soared. My feet turned into musical instruments as I used different parts of them to make a variety of sounds. It was such fun!

I was so lucky to have been taught by the best tappers in the world. They never missed a beat. They were always listening for clean, crisp tap sounds. They were so observant and precise. If I was doing a step wrong, they would immediately call out, "Do it again! Listen carefully to the sound! Don't stop until you get it right!" And I would keep trying the step until I got it right. I was fortunate to be trained under their watchful eyes.

As a beginning tapper, I would watch the older, more advanced student tappers. They inspired me. I copied some of their tap rhythms so I could be like them. But after a while, I discovered that tappers need to develop their own individual style. The way to achieve that is through what we call "improvisation."

Improvisation involves creating steps on the spot, in the spur of the moment. This style allowed me to bring the feelings in my heart into my dancing. As the music started to play and I connected with the beat, I used my feet to tell a story. I was free to express myself. My mind was not thinking about the steps. The steps came from deep within me, as my body seemed to move on its own. This kind of dancing is rather mysterious. But as a dancer, I have learned that the feelings derived from dance cannot be explained in words. That is why I need to dance!

At the dance studio, I was able to meet and make friends with many other dancers. I literally grew up with them on the dance floor. And although it was fun to express myself through improvisational solo dance, I also needed to dance with others as part of a team.

When we were dancing together, I felt like we were companions on the same journey. I learned to harmonize with others, as we moved together as one. I understood that I was part of something bigger than myself. I needed to resist thinking about my own style, because the success of the dance depended on all of us working together. It felt wonderful to dance with others this way. I experienced the beauty that comes from human cooperation and unity.

Dancing and creating harmony with my friends was easy. But, dancing with people I did not know well presented more of a challenge. My dance teachers taught me to get along with other dancers. They told me that I could not dance well if I was unfriendly. They warned me that such feelings bring about negative vibes in the dance. And they said audience members quickly pick up on such bad feelings.

At first, I did not believe this. I did not think getting along with every single dancer was important. But the first time I felt the slightest unfriendly feelings, I realized firsthand that it affected my dance. I knew it prevented me from dancing my best. From then on, I started to get along with everyone, and this made me a much better dancer.

My favorite thing about being a dancer is performing onstage in front of an audience. Nothing else compares to it! I have danced onstage so many times that it is like breathing for me: totally natural.

Developing the confidence that is needed to perform well took some time. In the beginning, I doubted myself. I used to think things like: "What if I forget the steps?" "What if I freeze out there?" When I thought like that, my muscles never worked right. Then when I went onstage, I was not able to give my best performance.

I needed to get rid of these thoughts. What I did was simple. Before going onstage, I would close my eyes and see myself performing the dance successfully. This helped me build confidence. I was now able to go onto the stage and do my best. After that, dancing onstage became a time of joy.

After years of training, I was finally ready to audition for Broadway shows in New York City. I auditioned for many parts. I got some parts. Others I did not.

My confidence was certainly challenged when I did not get a part. Rejection was hard to take. I used to get upset and cry. But I knew I could not walk away from my dream of being a dancer just because I got my feelings hurt. I had to pick myself up and keep going. I had to stop getting so upset.

I learned to see things differently: not getting a part was not so bad. Instead these became moments to learn from. It was an opportunity to go back into the studio to practice even harder to better myself as a dancer. And all this hard work enabled me to reach my true potential. I am grateful for these life challenges!

Now I am the teacher! As a dance teacher, I share with my students the wisdom from my life journey. Passing on the love of dance is the most wonderful thing I can do.

As I train my young students, I see them grow from beginning dancers, not too sure of themselves, into highly seasoned performers with well-developed artistic confidence and technique. I am their biggest fan!

As a dance teacher, I experience the power of dance daily as I watch my students flower as human beings. Each day, they are creating their own journey with dance just as I did. I am so fortunate to be a part of their journey, and I hope that they, too, will be forever dancing.